I Can Make
Nature
CRAFTS

written and photographed by

Mary Wallace

Owl Books

I Can Make Nature Crafts

Owl Books are published by Greey de Pencier Books Inc.,
179 John Street, Suite 500, Toronto, Ontario M5T 3G5

Owl and the Owl colophon are trademarks of Owl Communications.
Greey de Pencier Books Inc. is a licensed user of trademarks of Owl Communications.

Distributed in the United States by Firefly Books (U.S.) Inc.,
230 Fifth Avenue, Suite 1607, New York, NY 10001.

This book was published with the generous support of the Canada Council,
the Ontario Arts Council and the Ontario Publishing Centre.

Canadian Cataloguing in Publication Data

Wallace, Mary, 1950–
I can make nature crafts

ISBN 1-895688-48-5 (bound) ISBN 1-895688-49-3 (pbk.)

1. Nature craft – Juvenile literature. I. Title.

TT160.W35 1996   j745.5   C95-932252-3

Design & Art Direction: Julia Naimska

Crafts on the front cover, counterclockwise from upper left:
Grassy Head; Cornhusk Doll; Stone Statue; Nutty Buddies;
Twig Vase; Old-Time Writing; Burr Butterfly.

Other books by Mary Wallace
I Can Make Toys
I Can Make Puppets
I Can Make Gifts
I Can Make Games
I Can Make Costumes
How to Make Great Stuff to Wear
How to Make Great Stuff for Your Room

Printed in Hong Kong

A   B   C   D   E   F

CONTENTS

LET'S MAKE NATURE CRAFTS

You can make all the crafts in this book. It's easy. It's fun. These two pages show the things used to make the crafts in this book, but you can use other things if you like. You'll find most of what you need inside or outside around your house — get permission to use what you find. Pick only what you need, enjoy the natural setting, and have fun!

- corn silk
- cornhusks
- shallow bowl
- tempera paint
- cardboard
- googly eyes
- scissors
- crayons
- dandelion stems

- food color
- shallow dish
- moss
- shells
- small rag
- burr
- twist ties
- vegetable oil
- grass seed

4

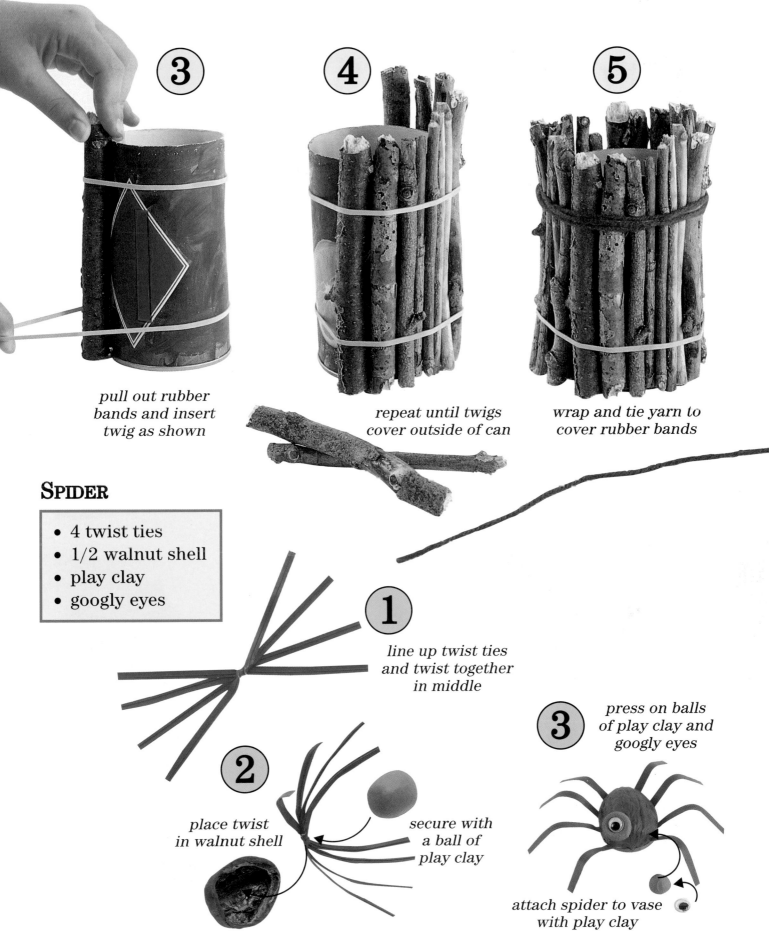

③ pull out rubber bands and insert twig as shown

④ repeat until twigs cover outside of can

⑤ wrap and tie yarn to cover rubber bands

SPIDER

- 4 twist ties
- 1/2 walnut shell
- play clay
- googly eyes

① line up twist ties and twist together in middle

② place twist in walnut shell

secure with a ball of play clay

③ press on balls of play clay and googly eyes

attach spider to vase with play clay

7

STONE STATUES

- small stones
- 1 spoon of vegetable oil
- bowl
- small rag
- play clay
- *decorate as you like*

dip tip of rag in oil and polish surface of stones

wipe off excess oil

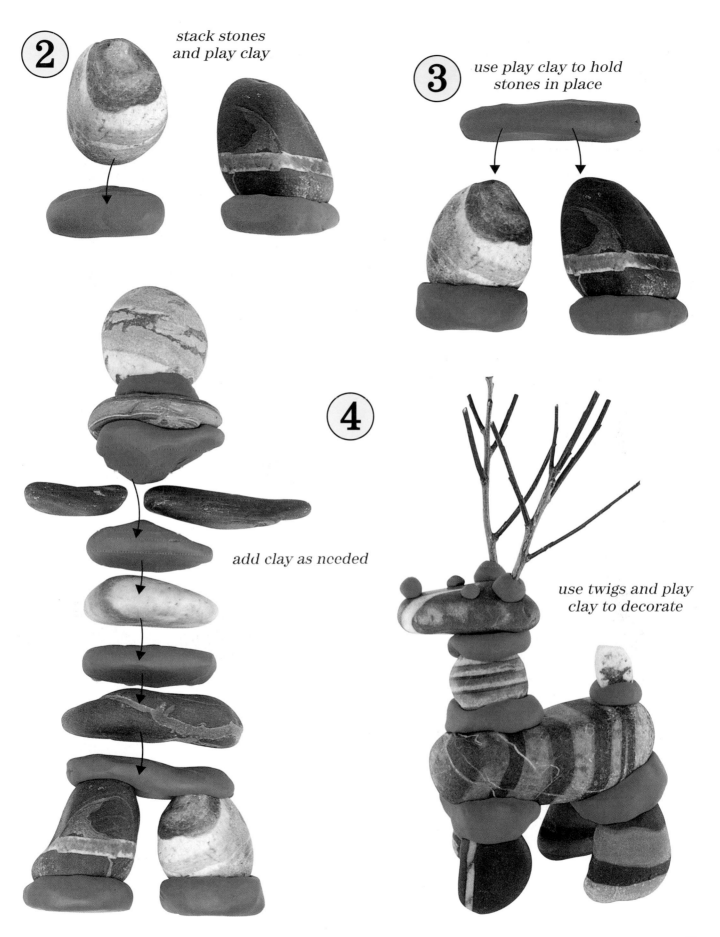

② *stack stones and play clay*

③ *use play clay to hold stones in place*

④ *add clay as needed*

use twigs and play clay to decorate

9

GRASSY HEAD

- stocking end
- potting soil
- twist ties
- rubber bands
- 2 googly eyes
- white glue
- 1 spoonful of grass seed
- shallow bowl
- scissors
- water

1

put several handfuls of soil in stocking end

2

shape soil into round head and close with twist tie

back of head

3

pinch soil in stocking to make nose and wrap with rubber band

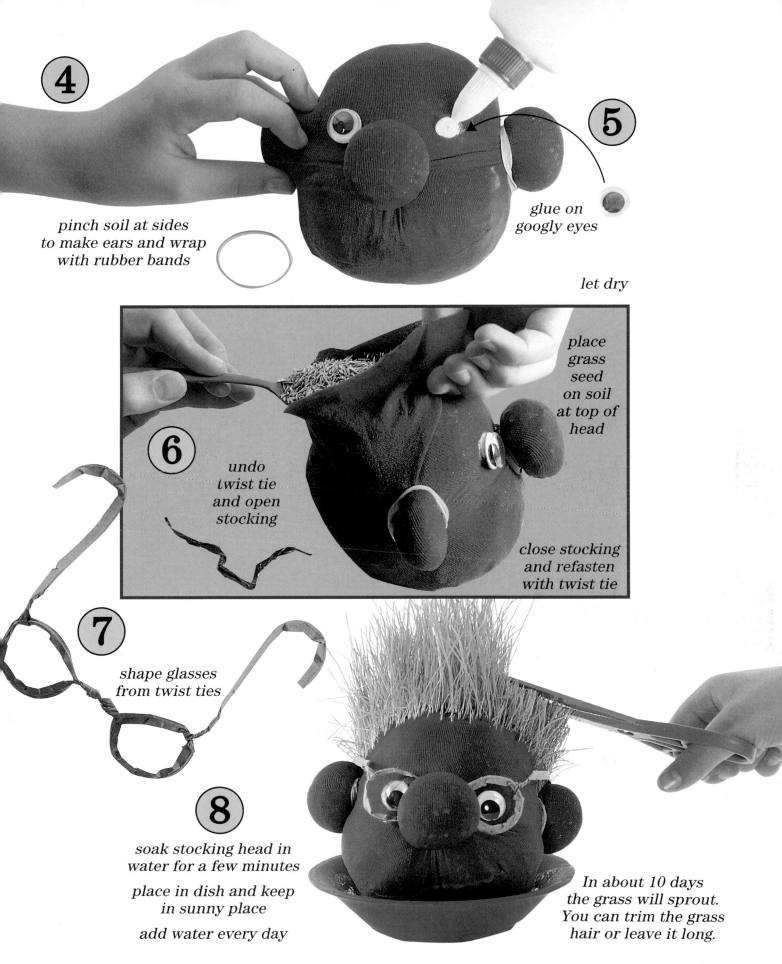

④ pinch soil at sides to make ears and wrap with rubber bands

⑤ glue on googly eyes

let dry

⑥ undo twist tie and open stocking

place grass seed on soil at top of head

close stocking and refasten with twist tie

⑦ shape glasses from twist ties

⑧ soak stocking head in water for a few minutes

place in dish and keep in sunny place

add water every day

In about 10 days the grass will sprout. You can trim the grass hair or leave it long.

NUTTY BUDDIES

- peanuts in the shell
- white glue
- twist ties
- scissors
- grass
- markers
- *decorate as you like*

①

crack peanut shell in half

save peanuts to eat later

②

glue along edges of both halves of shell

12

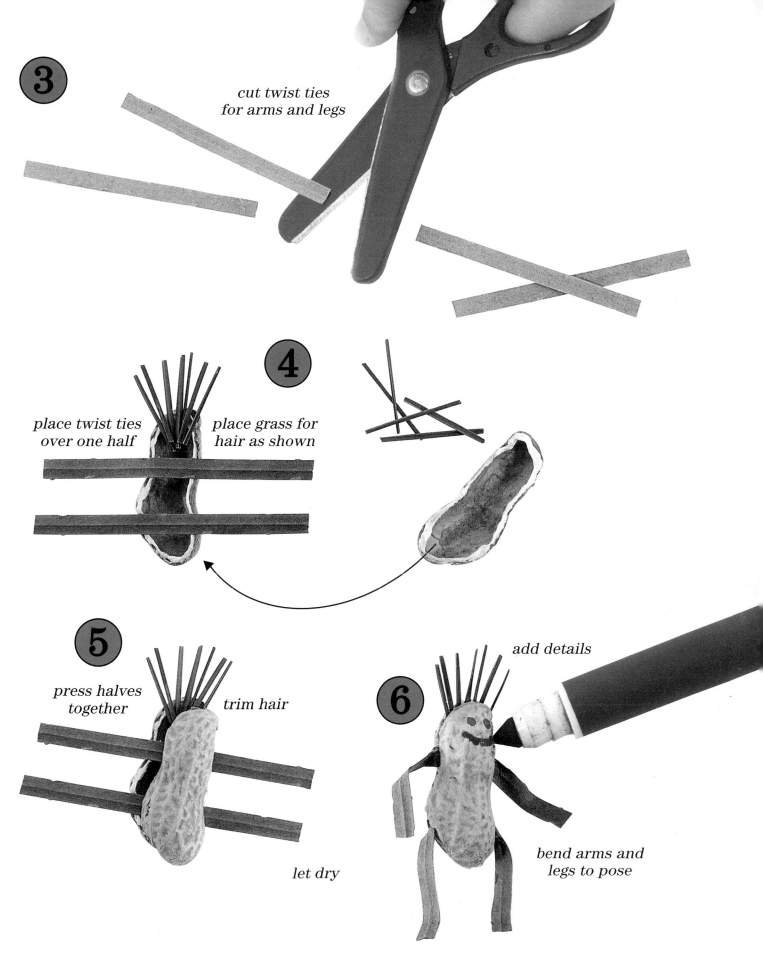

3

cut twist ties
for arms and legs

4

place twist ties
over one half

place grass for
hair as shown

5

press halves
together

trim hair

let dry

6

add details

bend arms and
legs to pose

PRESSED LEAVES

- grocery box
- scissors
- newspapers
- 2 large rubber bands
- tape
- fresh leaves
- *grown-up to help*
- *decorate as you like*

①

*ask a grown-up
to cut 2 pieces of
cardboard from box*

② *decorate as
you like*

③

*cut newspapers
to fit between cardboard*

4 stretch 2 rubber bands
around leaf press

tape rubber bands
along one edge

5 press leaves between
newspapcr

leave 4 sheets of newpaper
between each layer of leaves

close carefully and
use rubber bands
to hold closed

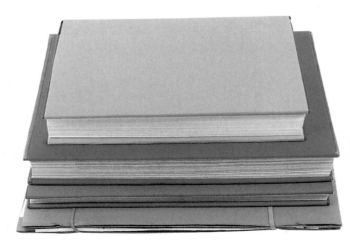

6 put closed leaf press
under a pile of books
for about 2 weeks

use pressed leaves
to decorate your other crafts

OLD-TIME WRITING

- found feather
- disinfectant
- scissors
- cardboard
- acrylic paint
- paintbrush
- pressed leaves
- white glue
- small jar with lid
- play clay
- drinking straw
- water
- food color
- *grown-up to help*

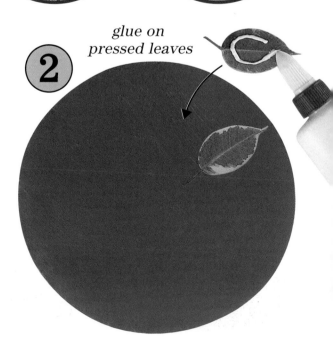

QUILL PEN

1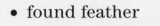

ask grown-up to clean
feather with disinfectant

cut off base at an angle

2 snip slit in point
with scissors

HOLDER

1 cut out circle
from cardboard

paint and
let dry

2 glue on
pressed leaves

For pressed leaves, see p. 14.

③ brush over whole surface with white glue

let dry

④ place jar in middle

glue clay to cardboard around base of jar

⑤ cut piece of straw to hold pen

⑥ glue down piece of clay and press in straw

INK

pour water and food color into jar

dip tip of quill pen then write

keep dipping as you write

17

GRASS WHISTLE

- a strong blade of grass
- your hands

1 *pick a sturdy blade of grass*

2 *hold grass taut between thumbs as shown*

cup your hands together

3 *press your lips against your thumbs and blow hard*

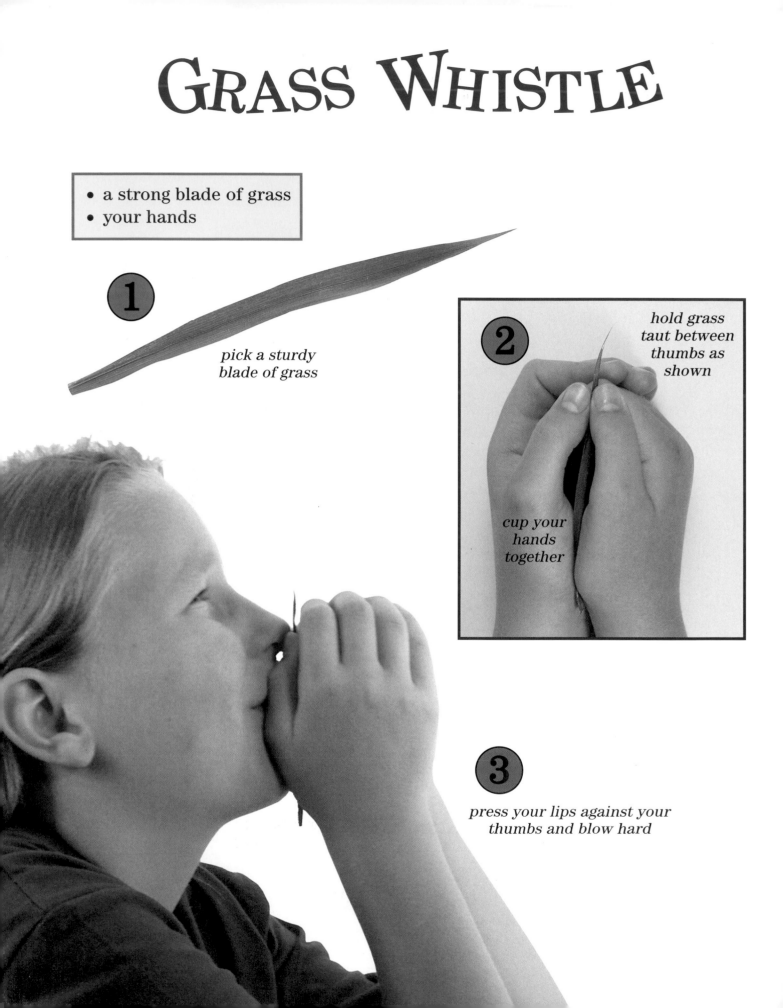

DANDELION LOOPS

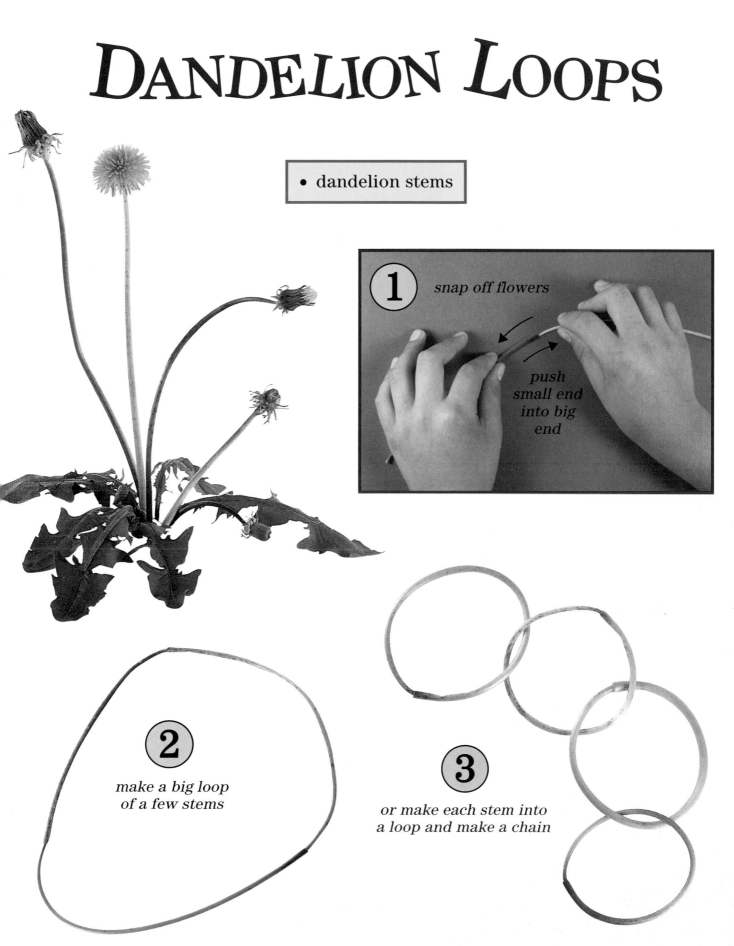

- dandelion stems

1 snap off flowers

push small end into big end

2 make a big loop of a few stems

3 or make each stem into a loop and make a chain

BURR BUTTERFLY

- paper
- pencil
- scissors
- crayons
- burr
- white glue
- *decorate both sides as you like*

①

fold paper in half

draw shape of butterfly wing

②

cut out

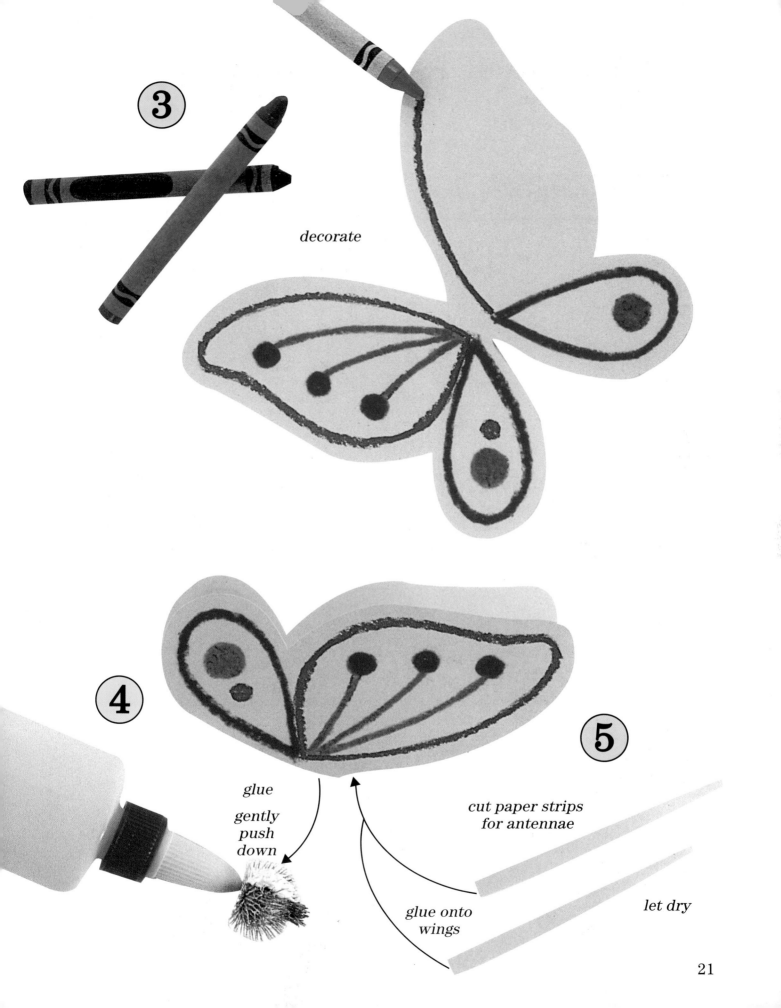

③

decorate

④ glue
gently
push
down

glue onto
wings

⑤

cut paper strips
for antennae

let dry

CORNHUSK DOLLS

- cornhusks and silk from raw ear of corn
- yarn
- scissors
- acrylic paint
- paintbrush

GREEN GIRL & BOY

1 save corn silk

pull husks off ear of corn

2 trim thick bottoms off husks

3 layer 3 husks

place corn silk across middle

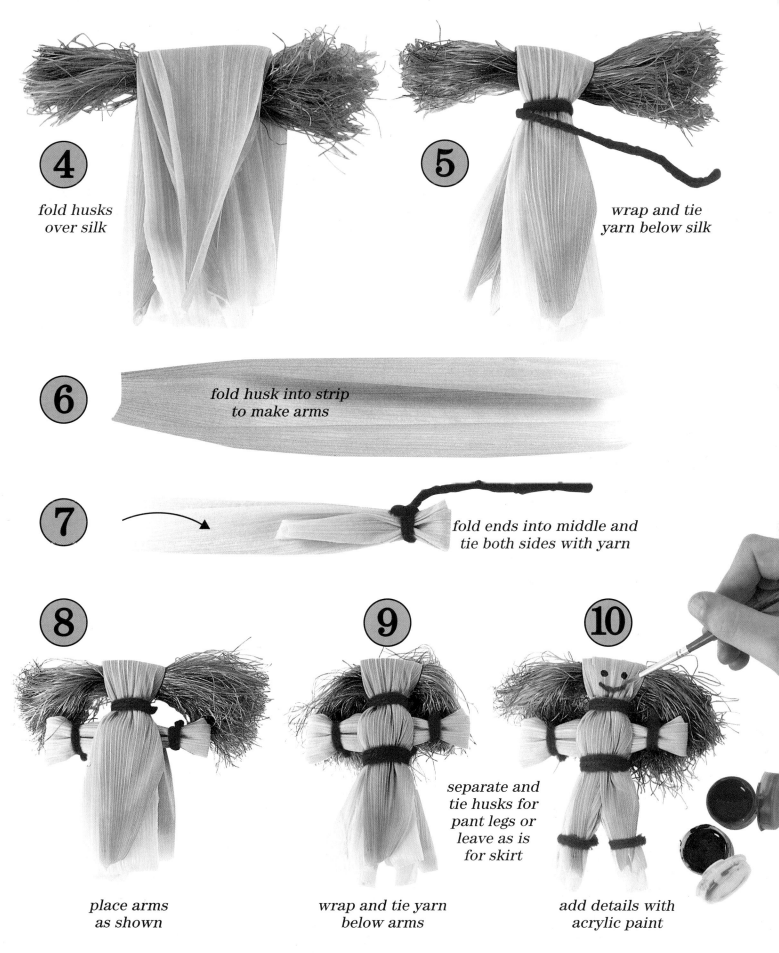

4 *fold husks over silk*

5 *wrap and tie yarn below silk*

6 *fold husk into strip to make arms*

7 *fold ends into middle and tie both sides with yarn*

8 *place arms as shown*

9 *wrap and tie yarn below arms*

10 *separate and tie husks for pant legs or leave as is for skirt*

add details with acrylic paint

23

DRIED DUO

- cornhusk dolls
- tempera paint
- water
- paintbrush
- scissors
- fabric
- yarn

1 cornhusks will dry from green to golden in about a week

2 color with tempera paint and water

let dry

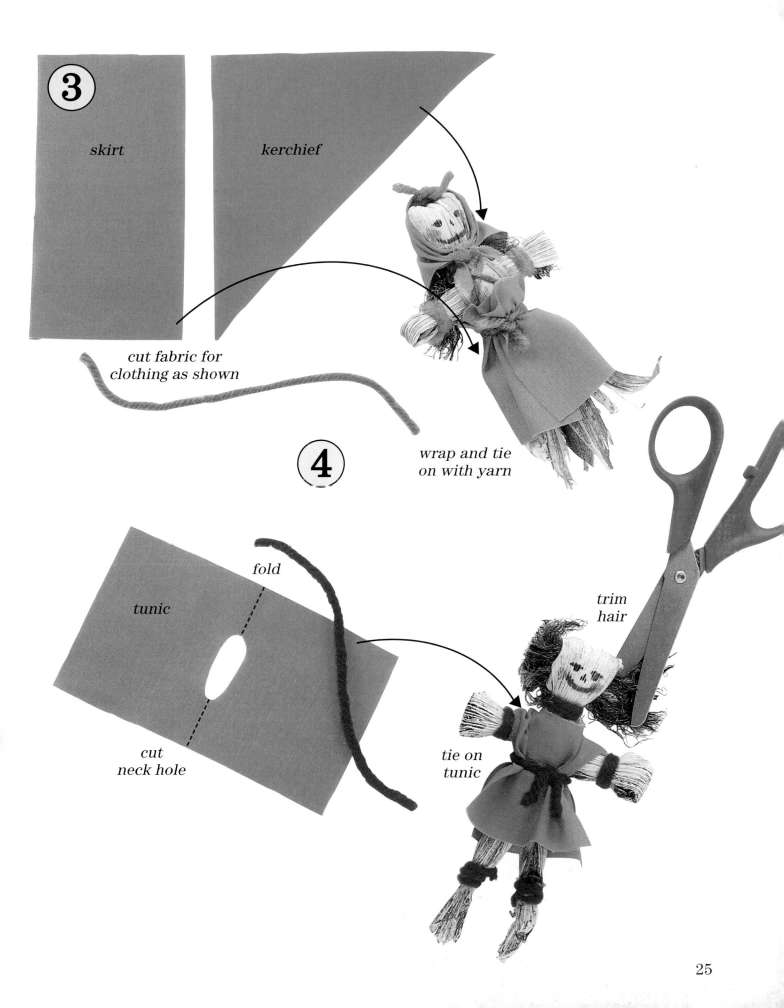

③

skirt

kerchief

cut fabric for
clothing as shown

wrap and tie
on with yarn

④

tunic

fold

cut
neck hole

tie on
tunic

trim
hair

MOSS GARDEN

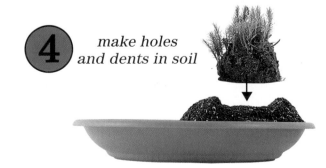

- several spoonfuls of moss
- potting soil
- shallow dish
- twigs
- stones
- shells
- water
- *decorate as you like*

1 collect moss from damp places among trees or along roadsides

2 fill shallow dish with potting soil

3 shape soil into valleys and hills

4 make holes and dents in soil

press in moss chunks

26

For Nutty Buddy, see p. 12.

5

push in twigs

add rocks and shells
to cover all soil

water lightly twice a week and
keep away from direct sunlight

FOREST FOLK

- twigs
- leaves and grass
- pine needles
- yarn
- scissors
- play clay
- acrylic paint and brush
- *decorate as you like*

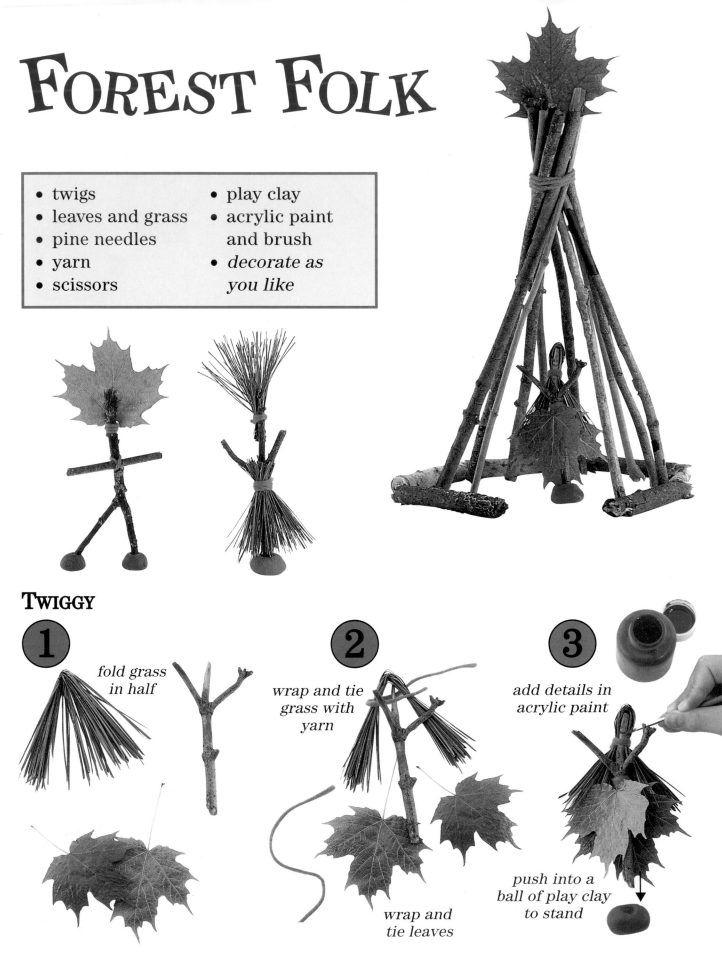

TWIGGY

1

fold grass in half

2

wrap and tie grass with yarn

wrap and tie leaves

3

add details in acrylic paint

push into a ball of play clay to stand

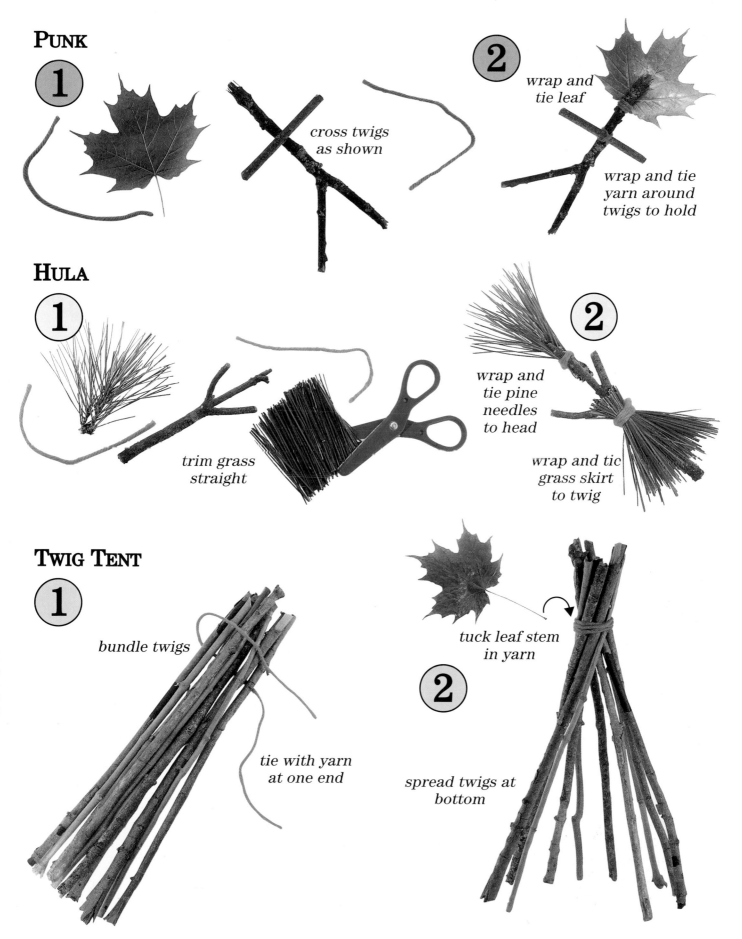

PUNK

1 cross twigs as shown

2 wrap and tie leaf

wrap and tie yarn around twigs to hold

HULA

1 trim grass straight

2 wrap and tie pine needles to head

wrap and tie grass skirt to twig

TWIG TENT

1 bundle twigs

tie with yarn at one end

2 tuck leaf stem in yarn

spread twigs at bottom

TREASURE TRUNK

- egg carton
- acrylic paint and brush
- cardboard
- scissors
- 3 spoonfuls fine sand
- 3 small containers
- food color
- white glue

 1

paint egg carton
with acrylic paint

let dry

2

cut cardboard
to fit top of
carton

3 put one spoonful
of sand in each
container

 4

mix food color
into sand

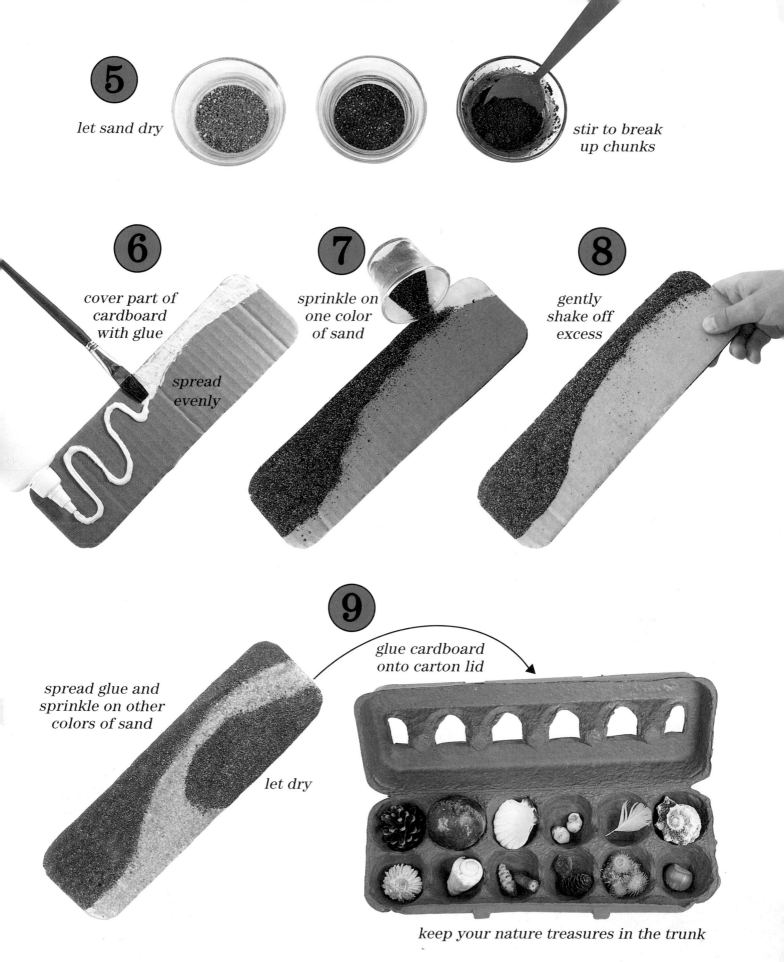

5 let sand dry

stir to break up chunks

6 cover part of cardboard with glue

spread evenly

7 sprinkle on one color of sand

8 gently shake off excess

9 spread glue and sprinkle on other colors of sand

let dry

glue cardboard onto carton lid

keep your nature treasures in the trunk

31

RESPECTING NATURE

- *Before collecting grass, moss, leaves, flowers or twigs, ask a grown-up to make sure they are not harmful.*
- *Don't eat wild berries unless a grown-up tells you they are not poisonous.*
- *Pick only small amounts of growing things. Pick only what you need.*
- *Don't pull a plant up by its roots.*

- *Never take all the leaves, flowers or seeds from a plant.*
- *If there are only a few plants of one kind growing, leave them alone.*
- *Sometimes it's better to just look, not pick . . . and take the memory home.*